"*Published With Jarvis* shows you exactly how to cut the time from writing a book from months (or years) to days (or hours)."

Dave Rogenmoser

PUBLISHED WITH JARVIS

SMASH THROUGH WRITER'S BLOCK TO GO FROM BLANK PAGE TO PUBLISHED IN 7 DAYS SUPER-POWERED BY AI

by
Darby Rollins
Zachariah Stratford

PUBLISHED WITH JARVIS

GO FROM BLANK PAGE TO PUBLISHED IN 7 DAYS WITH SUPERHUMAN ARTIFICIAL INTELLIGENCE

© 2021 JUNGLE ROCKET

All rights reserved. No portion of this book may be reproduced, stored in a retrieval system, or transmitted in any form or by any means—electronic, mechanical, photocopy, recording, scanning, or other—except for brief quotations in critical reviews or articles, without the prior written permission of the publisher.

Published in Austin, Texas by Jungle Rocket
www.JungleRocket.com

ISBN 978-1-7372968-0-5 hardcover
ISBN 978-1-7372968-1-2 paperback
ISBN 978-1-7372968-2-9 ebook

Cover design: César Pardo

To Jarvis, who reignited my passion for copywriting by helping me smash through years of writers' block to write and publish my first book in 72 hours.

To the team at Jarvis.ai for building a truly amazing, game-changing product that is empowering people around the world to find new and creative ways to use Jarvis to level-up their business and enhance their lives.

And to the entire #TeamJarvis community who have given me a reason to dive deeper into the inner workings of how to leverage artificial intelligence to make a lasting positive impact by exploring new ways to use this technology to write books, tell stories, and change the world.

CONTENTS

Introduction 9
Start Here 21
Day 1: Prepare 25
Day 2: Research, Outline & Format 36
Day 3: Write, Write, Write! 44
Day 4: Write, Write & Refine 50
Day 5: Write, Refine & Edit 69
Day 6: Refine, Edit & Design 73
Day 7: Click 'Publish' 79
Next Steps: The Finish Line? 92
Conclusion: Your Invitation 94
About The Authors 99
Acknowledgments 101

INTRODUCTION

"With great power, comes great responsibility."
Uncle Ben to Peter Parker in Spiderman

WANT TO WRITE A BOOK?

Join the club. There are millions of people who have always wanted to write a book but never seems to get around to it. The fact is, most books never make it past the would-be author's head and onto paper. This is because we can be so overwhelmed by all of the steps that need to be taken before we get into actually writing our story down on paper that we give up without even getting started. Every published author (and would-be published author) knows how daunting the task of writing a book from scratch can feel. But I'm here with some good news: there is one way to get over your fear of getting started and overcoming obstacles along the way—*Published With Jarvis*!

WHAT'S *PUBLISHED WITH JARVIS*?

Writing a book is a faster and far more credible way to gain recognition in your industry and be seen as the 'go-to' expert than posting a million videos to YouTube or cold-messaging 'prospects' until the cows come home.

Whether you're a published author or just beginning your journey, having a book will position you as an authority in your industry and build rapport with your target audience.

Published With Jarvis is for authors, entrepreneurs, writers, marketers, coaches, consultants, and experts who want to write, publish, and promote a book that positions them as an authority in their industry, establishes credibility, and generates leads to grow their business.

Published With Jarvis is ESPECIALLY for business owners who want to get their book OUT of their head and ON to paper.

If you've wanted to write a book for years but never had the time or were daunted by the task (rightfully so)...

There's a popular Chinese proverb that says: "The best time to plant a tree was 20 years ago. The second best time is now."

The best time to START writing your book is TODAY and a WELL POSITIONED BOOK is an asset you can leverage in your business to increase your authority, reputation, and influence with new customers and clients in any industry.

Your book brings your unique personality to life and delivers your expertise to the hands of prospects and readers who want to learn more about what you have to say.

It might be the BEST marketing asset you will produce for your brand and business…

Now, there's a process to writing books…

Be careful NOT to be distracted by all the shiny objects that steer you away from focus and get your book written, edited, published, and launched.

Published With Jarvis is an interactive book for action-taking authors or soon-to-be authors who harness the power of Jarvis and artificial intelligence to get their book out of their head and onto paper FAST.

THIS BOOK IS FOR YOU IF:
- "I want a book that builds authority in my field and industry."
- "I want a book that leads to more sales of my core offer."
- "I want a book that roadmaps my content for blog posts, videos, podcasts... anything."
- "I want a book because it's a personal challenge that you want to achieve." (ex. become a published author)
- "I want a book to nurture deep rapport with my audience."
- "I want a book that gets my story discovered by new audiences."
- "I want a book to land me more paid speaking engagements that increase my influence."
- "I want a book that leaves a legacy."
- "I want a book because _____."

There's a lot of reasons you might want a book. The way I see it, at the end of the day, a well-crafted book works for you 24/7 to generate leads into your business and prime ideal clients to show up banging down your door with their credit cards out ready to work with you.

Books are the cornerstone for positioning your unique offers to the market.

In my experience, the RIGHT offer, presented at the RIGHT time, to the RIGHT buyer, is the easiest sell in the world. Your book should do the hard work of marketing and pre-selling your offer, so that by the time a book buyer inquires about your services, they are already sold on what you have to offer and might only have a couple questions that can be answered through text, chat, or email.

Often I find business owners and entrepreneurs giving out time on their (or their sales teams) calendars for hour-long "discovery" calls or "strategy sessions" to close their big ticket offers.

The problem with this is that the folks (in my experience) who want their problem solved fast and have the money to pay for it, don't want to sit through an hour-long "discovery" call. Much less an hour long webinar pitch to get them on this call!

Again, I'm only speaking from my experience, but in today's 3-second world, people don't have time to hop on calls willy-nilly to get sold by a "high ticket closer".

The real 'Movers and Shakers' making things happen in the business world have an abundance of MONEY and understand that TIME is their most valuable asset.

(This is important for what we're going to be covering here, I promise)

Whether you are selling a $10 widget or a $50k mastermind, your book is going to put you and your offer in front of folks who have a decision to make: "Do I want to pay someone to help me solve this problem that I bought the book to help me better understand and solve… or am I going to do it on my own?"

There's a lot of folks who will take a book and run with it, execute, and reap the rewards.

There's also a lot of folks who will buy a book to gain insight into a process they know they need, and if the author of the books shows them step-by-step they can help them with their problem, they'd prefer to simply hire that person to solve their problem rather than spend the time, money, and energy doing it themselves.

Published With Jarvis shows you exactly HOW to write a nonfiction book FAST. What you do with it is up to you. Transparently, if you are the type of person who wants to work with the WHO that can get stuff done, we can help with that, too.

From writing to editing to formatting to publishing to selling and enrolling new clients into your big ticket offers…

That's what WE do, and the unbashful intention of this book is to provide so much value to you on the process we've developed alongside Jarvis that you are blown away and want to work with us at a higher level to build your Big Ticket Book Machine.

Inside **Big Ticket Book Machine**, we help you go beyond just publishing and actually get your book in the hands of your ideal clients while helping you sell more of your big ticket products and services.

I'll get off my soap box for now, but I wanted to get that out of the way so that we are on the same page. This book is going to give you the exact framework for getting it done on your own with the help of artificial intelligence to smash through writer's block and accelerate the process.

Just know we are here for you if you've got a big ticket offer that you want to use the book to sell more of. :-)

You can find out more about the Big Ticket Book Machine in the last chapter of this book.

Now, let's get back into the AI book writing side of the equation...

SKEPTICS, READ THIS:

I get it. You might be skeptical about the idea of writing a book with artificial intelligence, and rightfully so. This is some next-level shit!

- "I don't want to be replaced by robots."
- "It's too hard to find good content."
- "The readers will hate it because they're used to human authors."
- "Who is going to edit my work?"
- "What if the AI just plagiarizes other books?"

- "Writing a book is hard."
- "You can't be creative with AI."
- "The final product will be terrible."
- "It's not worth it."
- "I'm not sure if this is a good idea."
- "It's just a trend, it'll die out soon."
- "I don't want to be replaced by AI."
- "What about my privacy?"

As you can tell… I am not a skeptic about writing a book with AI. There are many benefits to using AI for writing books. It is the future of publishing and it will change everything. It's possible to use AI and humans together, but it's up to the author what they want to do. With this technology and our framework, you can write your book in days, not months or years—if you choose to accept the **7 Day Book Challenge**.

If you do your research and put in the work, your book will be more popular than you ever imagined because of tools like Jarvis and others mentioned in this book. Plus, you can still be creative with your book even if you're using AI—that's the whole point!

By the way, the questions above? I asked Jarvis what some of the questions a skeptic might say about writing a book with AI using the Blog Post Outline template in Jarvis.ai.

Did Jarvis strike a cord?

Love it or hate it, this is the future. How we harness the power of tools like Jarvis is up to us. Remember what Uncle Ben said to Peter Parker in *Spiderman*?

"With great power comes great responsibility."

HOW THIS BOOK IS DIFFERENT

Use this book as a step-by-step guide to focus on what YOU need to do each day of your **7 Day Book Challenge.**

The goal of this book, and **The 7 Day Book Challenge**, is not to have a PERFECT book… but a PUBLISHED book that is the **MVM (Minimum Viable Manuscript)** edition of your book that you can use to get into the hands of your Advanced Readers to give critical feedback on your book so that you can continue to refine and improve on your book NOW rather than putting it off for weeks, months, or years down the line.

By leveraging the power of Jarvis and this step-by-step system, you too can join the ranks of authors who are pioneering the process of writing and publishing books publishing books lightning fast—sometimes in 7 days or less!

You can read in order from front to back in less than an hour, but the time spent implementing the actions in this book is entirely up to you. You may find yourself referring back to Day 1 or Day 5 on the same day while you are making progress in your **7 Day Book Challenge**.

Use this book as a place to reference quickly and then get back to writing!

I recommend you set dedicated time aside during the week to focus on your book and block out all distraction. The less stress, the better. This book also comes with a community of AI authors for you to join and interact with during your process.

Ask questions, give more than you take, and respect everyone on this journey of writing books with Jarvis at **JarvisUnderground.com/Community**

Published With Jarvis is a 'living book' and will be updated on a constant basis to coincide with updates to Jarvis and acts as a hub for resources to tap into on an 'as needed' basis.

Yes, we are affiliates of many of the companies we recommend throughout this book. Most of our recommendations are industry standards in the book publishing business or have been personally tested and vetted during the development process of the book you hold in your hands now.

You can get access this list of ever-growing resources at **JarvisUnderground.com/Resources**

We coordinate and host live **7 Day Book Challenge**s for groups on a constant basis. The live challenges follow the structure laid out in this book and are where we continue to improve on the process and update this book. If you'd like to learn more or take **The 7 Day Book Challenge**, we invite you to join us for a week-long sprint that includes live calls and coaching on using Jarvis throughout this process. Visit **JarvisUnderground.com/Challenge** for more details.

HOW TO GET UPDATES TO THIS BOOK

This book WILL have more editions to come to it and because you have purchased a copy of *Published With Jarvis* now, you have access to all future digital editions as they are released. If you purchased on Amazon or received your digital version elsewhere and want to sign up for new releases, send an email to Hello@JarvisUnderground.com and we will get you on the list.

HISTORY OF THE 7 DAY BOOK CHALLENGE

The 7 Day Book Challenge started in January 2021 after *Published With Jarvis* co-author and course creator Darby Rollins wrote and published his first book, *Amazon Copywriting Secrets*, on Amazon in 72 hours using Jarvis from Jarvis.ai.

After showing the Jarvis.ai community how he did it, the first official **7 Day Book Challenge** was held and over a dozen books were written and published in one week.

Since then, Darby teamed up with Zachariah Stratford who is one of the Managing Partners at TheBookPatch.com which has been publishing since 2009, with over 60,000 books published, and millions of copies printed.

Working for years helping authors publish their books at TheBook.Patch.com, Zachariah saw first hand how difficult it is for people to actually hit the publish button and start selling their books.

The book *Published With Jarvis* and The **7 Day Book Challenge** are designed to accelerate the speed at which authors can deliver value to their readers and audiences.

CASE STUDIES

Here's what some of our past graduates are saying about their experience becoming published authors because they took the challenge:

Austin Distel, Author of 'Subscription Secrets'
Austin was a marketer in the SaaS industry until he wrote a book and published it on Amazon. Now, he's getting more leads, customers, and attention around his brand because he wrote the book on subscription in The 7 **Day Book Challenge**.

He even helped his dad become a published author by finally publishing his poetry book during a 7 **Day Book Challenge**!

"This is a life-long dream come true with my son." –Dad

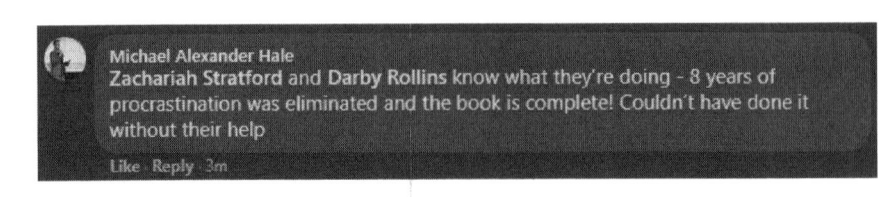

> **Michael Alexander Hale**
> Zachariah Stratford and Darby Rollins know what they're doing - 8 years of procrastination was eliminated and the book is complete! Couldn't have done it without their help
> Like · Reply · 3m

Michael Alexander Hale, Author of 'F*CK YOUR BS'
Michael took on a $1000+ bet over a decade ago with some friends to write a book in the next 7 years. He lost that bet... then more than a decade later he took The **7 Day Book Challenge** and became a published author in 7 days.

Cierra Leuck, Author of 'Not A Sales Book'
Cierra planned to write a book in 2020 but never got around to it. Then she took The **7 Day Book Challenge**, wrote and published her book on Amazon, and was flooded with leads asking for a copy of her book after she posted about it on Facebook... then THIS happened:

> Someone reached out to a person on my sales team about wanting the book.
>
> Then my sales guy booked a call with him and just made his first High Ticket sale because of the book.
>
> 😎
>
> Just thought you should know!

> cool! That 1 sale was worth $6800

18   Published With Jarvis

Natalie Tischler - 7 Day Challenge Grad
"Lifelong Dream Achieved"

"Writing book was always something I thought would be cool to do, but not until I was 50 or had "enough" expertise.

The 7 Day Book Challenge made it doable! It was like a "rip the Band-Aid off and JUST DO IT challenge!"

THE ALCHEMICAL CREATIVE PROCESS

Turn Your Ideas Into Progress and Impact Using the Four Elemental Steps of Creativity

NATALIE TISCHLER

Natalie Tischler, Author of 'The Alchemical Creative Process' Natalie always wanted to write a book and thought it would be cool to do, but was going to wait until she was older or had "enough" expertise… The **7 Day Book Challenge** made it doable! Natalie ripped off the Band-Aid and published her first book in just one week!

It Doesn't Stop There!

Every week, people are taking The **7 Day Book Challenge** and getting their book out of their head, on paper, and into the world with Javis.

WHY TAKE THE *PUBLISHED WITH JARVIS* 7 DAY BOOK CHALLENGE?

- ☐ Smash through writers' blocks and go from blank page to published in 7 days or less
- ☐ Slash the time to write a book from months to days with worksheets and templates that take the guesswork out of writing a book
- ☐ Whip your book out lightning fast with the help of Jarvis the AI writing assistant
- ☐ Jumpstart the book writing process with outline templates from best-selling authors
- ☐ Get clients, customers, and consulting gigs faster than ever because when people read your book they see you as the go-to expert
- ☐ Extract the book that's been sitting in your mind for years and finally hold it in your hand.
- ☐ Leverage your knowledge and productize it as a marketing asset that grows your business
- ☐ Bring your ideal customers to you on a silver platter by helping them solve a problem through your book

Ready?
Set?
Let's Go!

START HERE

"Alice asked the Cheshire Cat, who was sitting in a tree, "What road do I take?" The cat asked, "Where do you want to go?" "I don't know," Alice answered. "Then," said the cat, "it really doesn't matter, does it?"
Lewis Carroll, Alice in Wonderland

BEFORE YOU BEGIN...

Step 1: Sign-up for Jarvis.ai at WriteWithJarvis.com

Create an account with Jarvis.ai so you can leverage Jarvis to help write your book.

Jarvis.ai is the world's most powerful AI-writing assistant that helps authors and bloggers smash through writer's block and create high-quality content with ease. It can be used for any type of long-form text, from books to blogs to press releases to social media posts and beyond.

You can even use it to respond to book reviews!

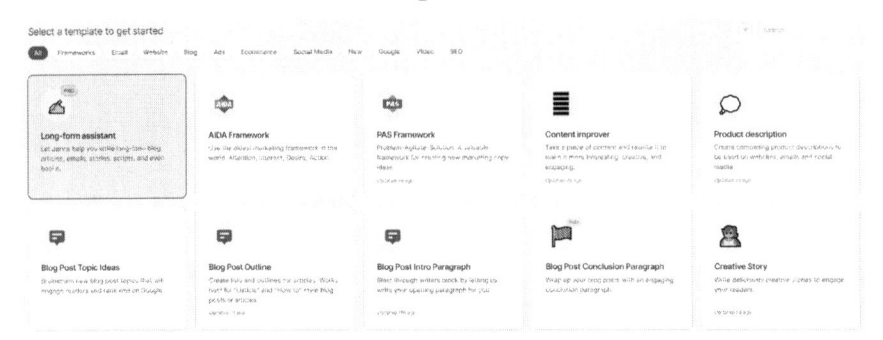

With their Pro Unlimited plan, you have an endless amount of credits to write with so you can use Jarvis without worry of running out of words. The Pro Unlimited plan also includes the Long-Form Content Assistant which revolutionized the way writers and authors have leveraged this AI tool in order to create long-form content quickly and easily.

In fact, much of the book you hold in your hands was written with the help of Jarvis.

You won't need to spend hours on end stuck starting at a blank page suffering from dreaded writers' block! And if that wasn't enough—we've worked out a special deal with the team.

They'll give you 10,000 FREE credits just by signing up today because you're reading this book! That way there are no limits on what you can achieve with Jarvis on your side.

Action: Go to WriteWithJarvis.com and get 10,000 FREE bonus credits when you sign-up today.

Step 2: Set the Topic of Your Book

Use these prompts to help you decide on a topic:
1. Brainstorm possible topics by making a list of things you are passionate about or have expertise in.
2. List out the pros and cons for each potential topic, and decide which one you would most like to write about that would be valuable to your audience.
3. Ask yourself what would be useful to others, or what problem can you solve in a step-by-step format?
4. Who is your target audience and how will this book help them with their problems or needs?

Pro Tip: If you are stuck between ideas, use the Blog Post Topic Ideas template in Jarvis.ai to help you brainstorm.

Step 3: Start Building Your Advanced Readers List & Curate Your 'Dream Team'

The goal of **The 7 Day Book Challenge** is to publish an MVM (Minimum Viable Manuscript) edition of your book that you can get feedback on from Advanced Readers and acts as a lead generator that attracts ideal clients and customers to your business. You want to list out the perfect people to get their hands on your book FIRST once it's ready to consume.

Action: Open a spreadsheet and start putting together a list of influencers in or out of your industry/niche that you want to make sure your book gets into their hands at all costs. These are often people in your professional network and close to it that are one or two degrees away from a referral to your book or business.

This list will be utilized once you publish your MVM and begin next steps to launching your book.

Now, let's get ready to dive into the *Published With Jarvis* 7 Day Book Challenge!

May the odds ever be in your favor...

NOTES

DAY 1
PREPARE

"Give me six hours to chop down a tree and I will spend the first four sharpening the axe."
Abraham Lincoln

WELCOME TO DAY 1!

Today, you're kicking off **The 7 Day Book Challenge** you've accepted to write and publish your book in one week.

This is where the foundation is laid for publishing your book and acts as a repeatable framework to build off as you continue refining your book until clicking 'publish'.

At the end of this chapter you will have a list of tools and resources that can be leveraged now and throughout the rest of the challenge.

While not all of these tools and resources are necessary, we'll give you a starting point to choose from FREE and PAID options that can each work to move your journey along and come back to you if you get stuck at any point of the process.

To make this as easy to reference as possible, we've put together a simple resource section that you can access and bookmark that includes this list of tools and resources AND provides other links to our communities and support group to join and ask questions during your **7 Day Book Challenge**.

To access these resources, please visit: www.JarvisUnderground.com/Resources

DAY 1 FOCUS
Timeblock Your Week

If you're an author or aspiring author, chances are that you've struggled with maintaining your focus on the task at hand—writing!

We all have those distractions that keep popping up and pulling us away from our work. But if we don't take responsibility for how to manage these distractions, they will continue to sabotage our productivity.

One key practice for improving productivity and getting more done in less time is called 'time-blocking.'

I'm going to share some of my tips for blocking off times during the week where you can go deep and focus on exactly what needs to be done in order to get serious about writing your book fast!

Tip 1) Block off specific times for research.

This might sound obvious, but when you are researching you are in a different state than when you are writing. It's important to separate your activities so they do not overlap and slow you down because your focus is split.

Tip 2) Block off specific times for writing

The time you block off for writing this week is going to be your most important, and given the context of **The 7 Day Book Challenge**, you'll need to take a close look at your schedule to determine where things fall in line.

If you work a traditional 9-5 job or have wacky hours, then you might not have much time during the day to work on your book aside from lunch or short breaks. If that's the case, put short sprints on your calendar during the workday where you know you will be able to focus on your book and keep the activities needed in this time to short, quick tasks that can be knocked out in 15-30 minutes. Example: Finding 10 quotes to incorporate into each chapter could fit into a 15-minute sprint.

Tip 3) Get up early and work on your book first thing in the morning. When we first wake up our brain is programmed to be a little bit more open and creative than at any other time during the day.

If you're like me, there is a lot of resistance to this. I find myself thinking things like "I'll just do it tomorrow" or getting sucked into Facebook or TikTok for hours and not making any progress with my writing

The truth is that if we want to get serious about our craft, this practice will absolutely be worth it because when you wake up early and block off time specifically for your creative pursuits, by default the rest of your day has room for other important tasks, too!

You might also be a night-owl and work best in the later hours—that's fine! Decide what part of your day your brain is most engaged and creative and build your writing schedule around that.

In addition to blocking off specific times during the week where you can go deep and focus on what needs done so as not to derail yourself from progress with the distractions of life, I also recommend blocking off entire days where you can focus on your writing pursuits to really focus on what needs done.

If you don't have plans this weekend, Saturday and Sunday might be the perfect days to block off entirely to get your book out!

Tip 4) Consider blocking off time to meet with an accountability partner or a coach if you need extra support in getting back on track. Join the Jarvis Underground community to find an accountability partner at JarvisUnderground.com/Community.

Tip 5) Plan what you will be working on during those blocks of time and set up reminders and alarms so that you're not tempted by other activities.

Tip 6) Batch your tasks when possible so that you can make the most productive use of time and don't create any more distractions.

Tip 7) Don't try to be perfect. Be prepared for blocks of time to get derailed by other things that come up, and also accept the fact that you're not going to finish drafting your book on day one of this plan—although it's possible!

Tip 8) Use the Pomodoro Technique.

When you write, do you have a system? Maybe you work in long blocks of time or maybe your approach is more sporadic. Regardless of whether your method is complex or simple, it's important that it works for you.

What if I told you there was an easy way to get more done with less effort? The Pomodoro Technique can help anyone increase their productivity and decrease the time they spend procrastinating.

The Pomodoro Technique comes from Francesco Cirillo and his timer that looked like a tomato. He invented this strategy back in the late 1980s. By breaking down tasks into 25 minutes intervals (called pomodoros), he found that he could tackle any project without feeling overwhelmed and getting distracted.

Some people find that the Pomodoro Technique is too rigid for them, but I've found it to be one of my most-used tools when it comes to writing a book (or any major project).

It helps you break your day into manageable chunks and feel like you're making progress at all times.

Find Your Accountability Partner

Finding a writing accountability partner can be tough, but it's worth the time and effort to find someone that you are compatible with. If you have trouble coming up with an idea or motivation to write, your partner will help keep you on track. Plus, if they are open to it, they can act as an editor once you begin writing. Here are some ways to find the perfect writing accountability partner!

Tip 1) Look for someone that you are compatible with. Try to find someone who is as passionate about writing as you and can help keep you motivated when the going gets tough… and it will.

Tip 2) Ask your friends, family members, or coworkers if they would be interested in being a partner. You may actually end up finding several people!

Tip 3) Search for a group or organization that meets in your area. There are many writing groups, clubs, and conferences out there where you can find an accountability partner to work with on the spot!

Tip 4) Post on your social media about your book so your friends and followers can help keep you on track. Even better, post in the Jarvis Underground community because we are all using Jarvis to write books and are here to support and lift each other up. We're all in this together!

These tips should get you started looking for the perfect writing accountability partner so that you stay motivated while completing your book!

Remember just because someone is not in this list does not mean they cannot offer support. There are many ways people give each other motivation when it comes to their goals and aspirations. Who doesn't want some free editing support?

It's worth asking around—don't forget about friends from high school or colleagues at work either—anyone could make the perfect partnership for what you're trying to accomplish—it might surprise you who stands out!

Complete These 4 Core Exercises

Before starting any project, especially one like writing a book, it's important to start with the end in mind.

These worksheets/exercises are designed to help lay the foundation for your book before you get to writing so as roadblocks come up (and they will) you can refer back to them and regain clarity on your mission.

You can access digital versions of each worksheet at JarvisUnderground.com/Resources.

Know Your Why
Ask yourself: "Why am I doing this?"

Don't give me a generic answer... I want you to really dig deep here. What caused you to join this challenge?
Ask yourself: "Why will they read?"

Again, I want you to dig deep. What value are you bringing to your readers? How will you change peoples lives?

Set Your Goals
Ask yourself: "What is the impact this book will have on your audience?"

Think of this in terms of what is the ultimate goal for your readers?
Ask yourself: "What goals do you have for yourself?"

In terms of sales, what are your goals? It's OK to want to do well and make a lot of sales.
How many sales do you want:
- During Launch Week?
    - ⇨ Tip: A good number to shoot for would be 150-250 copies. I don't mind you thinking big though!

- During Your First Quarter?
    - ⇨ Tip: 500 copies in your first quarter is a great target. Again be optimistic and somewhat realistic.
- During Your First Year?
    - ⇨ Tip: 1000 is a great target! You can do just about anything with 1000 fans.

Ask yourself: "What are my long term goals?"

How do you want this book to affect your career 2-5 years down the road?

You may want to have courses, or coaching, or a series of books with other products...

Define Your Avatar

Write out exactly WHO your ideal reader is. You will be speaking to them throughout this book, so the more clear you are on who they are, the more your message will get across. Keep in mind, you might have several 'avatars' and may need to repeat this exercise multiple times to capture each of your readers' personas.

What's Their Basic Info?
- Name
- Age
- Marital Status
- Children?
- Location
- Favorite Quote
- Occupation
- Annual Income
- Job Title
- Level of Education

What are their Goals and Values?
- Write down their goals, values, dreams and desires

Where do they get their sources of information?
- Write out your reader gets their sources of info in the categories of:
  - Books
  - Magazines
  - Blogs/Websites
  - Conferences
  - Gurus

What are their challenges and pain points?
- Write out what obstacles, challenges, and present pain points your reader is going through when they pick up your book
  - What daily challenges do they face when they are attempting to achieve their goals?

What are their possible objections?
- What objections or questions might your reader have when it comes to purchasing your book or believing the information you are giving them?

Find Your Spine

This is the step between your Goals and creating your Outline.

Ask yourself: Why am I uniquely qualified?
- Take at least three answers from your why and list them here. Try and see if you can make them at least a page. Remember, you can list qualifications (lessons from mentors) and experiences (stories/lessons from life) to flesh it out and make it more interesting.

Ask yourself: Who is my book helping?
- Take at least three examples of the types of people you can help and list them here. Try to imagine different

versions of your ideal customer. For example, if you want to help dads, is it just young dads, or can single dads also use your advice? If you want to help people get in touch with their creative side, are you working with beginners or someone experienced? Musicians? Photographers?

Ask yourself: What will my reader achieve?
- Write three examples about what the readers will achieve and how that will feel for each of the people above.

Ask yourself: How does this book help them achieve that?
- Now we are getting to the good stuff! List the how of your book with either "The Hero's Journey Outline" or the "Problem Solving Outline" that you will find in Day 2.
  - When I started, my life looked like this…
  - Then I did this…
  - Then this happened…
  - And so on...

Action: Open a Google Doc or journal and write out your answers to each question/prompt from above.

CHALLENGE RESOURCES

This is a short list of the main tools we will be using to write your manuscript with. If you use another tool or find something cool that you've used in your writing experience, let us know and share it with the group! We're always on the lookout for the best tools to help people through the challenge.
- Jarvis Underground FREE Facebook Community (JarvisUnderground.com/Community)
- Jarvis.ai (Sign-up at WriteWithJarvis.com for 10,000 BONUS credits)
- Google Docs and Sheets (Writing and Research)

- Grammarly (Spelling, Sentence Structure)
- 4 Core Worksheets (JarvisUnderground.com/Resources)

More resources can be found at the end of each day throughout the challenge, and on our ever-growing resource list at JarvisUnderground.com/Resources.

DAY 1 ACTION STEPS
- Timeblock your week
- Find your accountability partner
- Post about your journey on social media
- Sign-up for Jarvis.ai at WriteWithJarvis.com
- Complete the worksheets and exercises above
- Watch 'Bonus Videos' in JarvisUnderground.com/Resources

NOTES

DAY 2

RESEARCH, OUTLINE & FORMAT

"If we knew what we were doing, it would not be called research, would it?"
Albert Einstein

WELCOME TO DAY 2!

Today we're talking about outlining your book, the editing you may need, and continuing any research needed to build your book's foundation.

Because you purchased this book, we've included a bonus training on book research and outlining.

This masterclass is presented by elite ghostwriter and publisher of over 300+ bestselling books, Matthew Thrush.

You do not want to miss out on watching this today as this masterclass contains the same secrets and processes Matthew charges his private clients big money to do for them.

DAY 2 FOCUS

Today, you want to focus on researching your market, understand the best categories for you to release your book into, and what is going into the outline of your book.

Research

There are plenty of research tools out there to make sure your book is structured properly and placed in the right category to be found by the right readers. Some free, some paid.

Here are a few of each that can help validate your book as people search for answers you will address in your book (and make sure that your chapter titles and subtitles are SEO friendly so search engines like Amazon and Google index your digital version to show up in the search results. You can find these and a more extensive list of research tools at **JarvisUnderground.com/Resources**

- Amazon's search bar (free)
- KDSpy (paid)
- Answer the People (paid)
- Publisher Rocket (paid)
- Google Docs and Sheets (free)
- Jarvis.ai (paid)

PRO TIP: Use Jarvis as a sounding board to expand on the outline for speed and perspective.

*Note that the research done here can be used for your cover design when you or a designer gets to that during the challenge.

Outline

Use these outline templates below as time-tested sources of truth that are the foundation of novels and bestsellers. These pair well with Matthew Thrush's masterclass training.

The problem solving outline walks the customer step-by-step through the problem they face. You are the guide, and by being a guide who uses stories, your message will land with your reader and have a greater impact.

For nonfiction books in particular, your book should have a clear outcome for the reader. You identify that outcome and create stories to walk the reader through each chapter. You'll find a mixture of the 'Hero's Journey' outline in every story, especially stories that get remembered. Authors need their readers to remember them.

What better way than to give massive value than by helping your reader solve a real problem, and present them with further solutions and options if they want to pursue more with you? These outlines combined make for the perfect-storm of outlining and writing a #1 bestseller, even if that's not your intention.

These templates are followed by the bestselling authors and publishing houses including that of Matthew Thrush, who's 90-minute masterclass goes over his process for writing over 300+ bestsellers.

Outline 1) The Non-Fiction Bestseller Problem Solving Outline

Problem Solving Outline
First Answer these 5 questions then fill out the outline, try to include at least 3 sub-points for each chapter.
- What? What is the concept, topic, or idea you want to relate to the reader?
- Where? Where does this concept, topic, or idea, apply?
- Why? Why does this matter?
- Who? Who is this for, or who is involved?
- When? Is there a concept of time involved?
- How? How will this happen?

Title
Subtitle
Introduction
Chapters

Chapter 1: Problem you are solving.
Why is it important to solve this problem?
A)
B)
C)

Chapter 2: History of the problem
Where did it all start? Where are we now?
A)
B)
C)

Chapter 3: Your Method for Creating this Change
Why is your method different?

Chapters 4–9: Additional Steps For Creating Change
- What do we need to do first?
- Second?
- Third?
- Chapter 10: What the Future Holds
- Conclusion
- 5-7 answers you covered in the book

Research and Resources
List all the tools needed for the journey.

Outline 2) The Rapid Problem Solving Outline Recipe

The Rapid Problem Solving Outline Recipe
- (1 minute) Grab 'egg timer' (or phone timer, watch timer... any timer)
- (1 minute) Open Blank Page
- (2 minutes) 1st step—title and paragraph
- (2 minutes) 12-16 Topics you're going to cover
- (2 minutes) Organize topics
- (7 minutes) 4 things you'll talk about in each chapter

Polish & Go

Jarvis Pro Tip: Templates to Use
- Blog Post Topic Ideas (Chapter/Topic Ideas)
- Blog Post Outline (Chapter/Topic Ideas)
- Blog Post Intro Paragraph (Expand on Topic or Blub/About)
- Perfect Headline (Title)
- Sub-Headline (Sub-Title)
- Product Description (Blurb)

You can also use the Long-Form Assistant to play with Title and Intro Paragraphs. Once you get a title and paragraph about the book, open the Power Editor mode so you can mix in the templates above.

Outline 3) The Hero's Journey

The Hero's Journey
It is commonly agreed that Joseph Campbell's book The Hero With a Thousand Faces has served as the framework of many popular films and books.

Such works include: "Star Wars", "Harry Potter", "The Hunger Games", and more.

Your outline is a guide that helps you organize thoughts and does not restrain the way you want to write. Your readers will discover your book as they read it, which is why I included this Hero's Journey outline to help orient you as you build your story and guide your reader on a journey through your book.

The Hero's Journey Outline
Introduction: 5-7 questions you will answer in the book
Chapter:
1. The Ordinary World.
    a. At one time you were like other mere mortals, tell us about that.
2. The Call to Adventure.
    a. You knew things could be different, tell us about that.
3. Refusal of the Call.
    a. What will happen if they don't? Maybe you had doubts, maybe others told you it was impossible, tell us about that.
4. Meeting the Mentor.
    a. Someone or something inspired you to believe differently, tell us about that.
5. Crossing the Threshold.
    a. You decided to take that first step, tell us about that.
6. Tests, Allies, and Enemies.
    a. What was your first difficult lesson, who helped and who discouraged your progress?
7. The Innermost Cave.
    a. A terrible danger or inner doubt you finally had to overcome, tell us about it.

8. Supreme Ordeal.
    a. The final test you overcame.
9. Reward.
    a. Success! Revel in it!
10. The Road Back.
    a. You have gained wisdom and now need to share it.
11. Resurrection.
    a. The hero has become a guide, tell us about it.

Conclusion: 5-7 answers you covered in the book

Research and Resources

Format

Through your research you should determine the best size and format of your book. Determine your format now and follow this in your outline and book creation to save time down the road.

There are formatting softwares you can use, both free and paid. You can also hire people who specialize in formatting if you'd rather not do the work. Either way, figure out the game-plan now so you are prepared to keep moving forward as we approach Day 7 and don't get bogged down by things that could have been prevented.

We go fast at light here to start, which is why Google Docs is how I start a manuscript. For making your interior reflect your brand and offer more than a simple Doc can do, we've included some resources to formatting and editing softwares you can review at **JarvisUnderground.com/Resources**

DAY 2 ACTION STEPS

1. Watch Matthew Thrush's masterclass
2. Dig deep into the research, leave no stone unturned.
3. Create your outline using your research and Jarvis to help with any roadblock or to spark some creativity

NOTES

DAY 3

WRITE, WRITE, WRITE!

"Concentrate all your thoughts upon the work at hand. The sun's rays do not burn until brought to a focus."
Alexander Graham Bell

WELCOME TO DAY 3!

Today, we're going to be talking about writing and editing your book as you move forward now through your **7 Day Book Challenge**.

Often, the editing process can take more time in the development of a book than the actual writing itself!

That was my experience, anyway. I knocked out the core of my content for my first book in the first 12 hours of writing and then the rest of the 72 hours was spent editing, formatting, and designing the cover.

This is your time to shine with Jarvis and start getting your book onto paper.

Once you tap into flow with Jarvis, you'll be AMAZED at the speed you can write (or spend less time staring at a screen NOT writing because of your writers' block)...

But just because we're focusing heavily on writing today does not give you the luxury to ignore the fact that you or somebody will be editing your book at some point.

Be aware of the fact that we are going to need editing as your book develops over time so that you can save more time by being conscious of your words and storyline.

Types Of Non-Fiction Editing To Be Aware Of:

- Developmental Editors
- Content Editors
- Copy Editors
- Proofreaders

Developmental Editors

Developmental editors are responsible for making sure that a book is well written and has the potential to be published. A developmental editor will read through your manuscript, looking at things like plot, character development, dialogue, and so on. Developmental editing helps authors take their writing to the next level by providing feedback as well as suggestions for changes in order to make the writing more engaging.

Content Editors

As the name suggests, a content editor is someone who edits and improves the quality of your writing. They are responsible for making sure that everything you write sounds good to readers. A content editor will also make sure that your ideas flow smoothly from one sentence to the next so that it's easier for people to read what you have written. Content editors can be found in many industries but they play an essential role in non-fiction books where there may not be a lot of material available on certain topics.

Copy Editors

Copy editors are hired by authors to check grammar, spelling, punctuation, and formatting errors in their work. They also ensure that the author has followed all of the conventions of standard written English such as capitalizing proper nouns and use of hyphens or en dashes where appropriate.

In some cases they will request changes be made to sentences which might not follow present tense rules or would otherwise change the meaning of what was being said.

Proofreaders

Have you ever written a book and thought it was perfect? It's not! You need a proofreader—a second set of eyes. Nonfiction books are usually about true stories, so the details have to be correct. A proofreader is someone who goes through your nonfiction book for errors in spelling, grammar, and punctuation. These errors can make readers think that you don't know what you're talking about or your facts are wrong. A good proofreader will catch these mistakes before they get published!

So now you know a bit about editing, enough to know that the better your grammar, sentence structure, and storylines make sense to the reader, the less editing you will need!

Something to keep in mind while you move through the challenge, but don't let the thought of it hold you up! Right now though, more important than the editing is getting the words on the paper, so that's what we're going to be focusing on today: write, write, write!

DAY 3 FOCUS

Today our focus is getting your book out of your head and onto paper.

It could be in your head, or somewhere else.

Maybe you've got a book buried in PowerPoint presentations, in podcasts, or recordings from live events. Maybe it's just in your head and you need to get out.

You've already done the hard part, which is outlining your book and getting clear on your goals for what you're about to do—time for the fun part and start writing!

If you feel stuck, if you feel like you're just really struggling to even work with Jarvis, go ahead and pull open your phone, open up the app and download Otter AI or use a voice podcast editing tool like Descript. (or if you have another voice-to-text app you prefer, go at it!)

Voice-to-text has evolved a lot over the last few years, and along with the advancements in artificial intelligence, it's giving people the superpower to 'speak books'.

When speaking a book, imagine walking your customer along the journey you've mapped out in your outline. Once spoken, you can upload your recording to Google docs. Then, copy the parts you want to edit and expand on, and paste them into Jarvis.ai's Long-Form Assistant so you can tap into Jarvis to help edit, rephrase, make more creative, and much more in Power Mode. (We talk about this in Day 4)

Pro Tip: Use Jarvis to simplify text, edit and expand on topics!

DAY 3 RESOURCES

Jarvis will get in a good flow of your story and what you're trying to get across. If you're using him as an assistant that you're bouncing ideas off of and building on top of what he is saying, you might run into some repeated words or sentences. Now there's a few different ways that you can do this you can use the *** and ## signs to control more of Jarvis' focus.

We've added a list of shortcuts and tricks for using Jarvis you can access for free at **JarvisUnderground.com/Resources**.

All things said and done, today you're off to the races! You should have your outline in front of you, you should have your avatar and goals completed from Day 1 and Day 2 and are set up for success as we move forward in the challenge.

DAY 3 ACTION STEPS

Open up your Google Doc (or whatever program you're going to be writing in), open up Jarvis... and start writing! Build momentum off the outline and get the words out.

If you feel stuck or if you get stuck, pull up your phone, or use a voice-to-text transcription software, such as Otter, Descript, Voice In, and/or Google Speech-to-Text.

Get the meat of your content out as much as you can today, and if you've got 10 extra minutes, I suggest watching Austin Distel's video on how to make the perfect nonfiction book introduction in our resources section at **JarvisUnderground.com/Resources.**

NOTES

DAY 4

WRITE, WRITE, REFINE!

"I don't care how much power, brilliance or energy you have, if you don't harness it and focus it on a specific target, and hold it there you're never going to accomplish as much as your ability warrants."
Zig Ziglar

WELCOME TO DAY 4!

Today you're writing, writing, and writing some more! Refine as you go, and maintain focus. Eyes on the prize and move the needle closer to the finish line!

DAY 4 FOCUS

Today, make sure you're staying organized and focused on the task at hand. Continue to write and get those words out of your head, get them onto paper with Jarvis.

Many of the challenge grads used this time to continue getting the 'meat and potatoes' of their book done—the stuff that Jarvis can help you with at lightning-speed inside the Long-Form Assistant.

While you are writing, make sure you are refining as you go. Javis can be a great help here with templates like Content Improver that take what you wrote and help make it better... or at least from a different perspective.

Ask Jarvis to help you out a little bit if you feel content is a little too complex, try using the Explain It To A Child template to make your words simpler and easy to digest. It's recommended to write at a 5th-6th grade reading level... at least that's what my experience and the internet tells me.

If you're feeling stuck on where to start to open up a story, leverage The Hero's Journey template from before to tap into the power of storytelling. You could also use Jarvis inside the 'Creative Story' template to help get those creative juices flowing!

If you're opening up a thought or struggling to start a paragraph, try using Jarvis and the Blog Post Intro Paragraph or continue your story inside the Long-Form Assistant and simply keep asking Jarvis for re-phrases and creative inspiration to your text to make them come to life!

If that doesn't help kickstart your creativity, pick up the mic and record. Speak your book then edit it shortly afterwards. Descript is a great tool for this!

You can also leverage Jarvis as a 'micro-editor' to rephrase and correct run-on sentences, or remove words like 'um, uh, like' if they are repeated. Remember Jarvis isn't perfect here, but if it's minor and you don't want to retype everything yourself or just want to let Jarvis do more work for you... all you need to do is click a button and the next idea comes out.

Isn't it great to have such a nice personal writing assistant right next to you, for inspiration and carrying the load literally whenever you want? Especially the Long-Form Assistant...

What a game-changer!

Inside Long-Form Assistant you'll see two types of modes:
- Focus Mode
- Power Mode

Focus Mode is great for just that... FOCUS! It is an ever expanding tool that help you write out your content without any distraction from other tools inside Jarvis.ai.

While I'm a fan of Focus Mode, if you REALLY want to see Jarvis work, open up Power Mode.

On the left side, you'll be able to switch between all the different templates Jarvis has to offer.

The thing every new user of Jarvis needs to understand is that your input direction is critical to the outputs you receive. Using the templates above aren't always going to work the first try, or at all if the input is confusing and not clear for what the output should be, ideally.

There's a lot of templates, too... so it's important to understand what they do while also looking at ways to get creative and use the "intended use" for your desired outcome. Jarvis brings a lot of inspiration and creativity to the table with just a little help in the right direction from you.

Use the following templates and their 'intended use' as guidelines and think about ways you could use a tool with this 'intended us' to write your book and also how they can help sell your book when it comes time to start promoting.

Jarvis.ai Templates (And What They Do)

Disclaimer: This is by no means a comprehensive list of all the templates inside Jarvis.ai, but it's the main ones I have used in writing my books with Jarvis. Explore all the various templates at WriteWithJarvis.com—new ones are being added every week!

AIDA Framework
Use the oldest marketing framework in the world. Attention, Interest, Desire, Action.

Input: The Step By Step System to go from blank page to published in 7 days using Jarvis and artificial intelligence. This book outlines the framework that helps people publish books lightning fast and get their book out of their head and on paper

Output:

Attention: Struggling to write a book?

Interest: Writing With Jarvis is the only course that will show you how to go from blank page to published in 7 days using artificial intelligence. This system outlines the framework that helps people publish books lightning fast and get their book out of their head and on paper. It's time for you to take action and start writing your story today!

Desire: You deserve more than just an idea, you deserve a finished product. Get started with this easy-to-follow guide today by clicking on this ad right now!
Action: Click here for more information about Writing With Jarvis or click here to purchase it now!

PAS Framework
Problem-Agitate-Solution. A valuable framework for creating new marketing copy ideas.

Input: The Step By Step System to go from blank page to published in 7 days using Jarvis and artificial intelligence. This book outlines the framework that helps people publish books lightning fast and get their book out of their head and on paper

Tone of Voice: Smart, 5th grade level

Problem: Writing is one of the most challenging things for people to do. Whether you're writing a book or an article, it can be hard to get started and even harder to finish.

Agitate: Most writers say that they have a lot of ideas but never end up doing anything with them because they don't know how to start or where to go from there. Even worse, some people write their entire book only once then spend months trying to find someone who wants to publish it!

Solution: The solution is simple—follow the proven framework outlined in this book and watch your productivity skyrocket! In just 7 days you'll learn how I went from blank page zero (and no idea what I was going to write about) all the way through publishing my first best selling book in less than 1 month using these principles. By following this process, you'll finally be able create something out of nothing and get your work done fast while still making sure that it's high quality work

Product Description
Create compelling product descriptions to be used on websites, emails and social media.

Input: The Step By Step System to go from blank page to published in 7 days using Jarvis and artificial intelligence. This book outlines the framework that helps people publish books lightning fast and get their book out of their head and on paper

Output:
In the book *Published With Jarvis*, you will focus on your project during every daily meeting until it's completed. You will be able to use artificial intelligence, Jarvis' software program that helps people write a book in 7 days or less, so life doesn't interrupt your flow and keep you from finishing it.

"No more pretending you want to write, when really you don't. You're not just writing anymore; your words are manifesting into something beautiful."—Writer's Block Buster

So you have a story inside of your head? It's time to get it out, then. Get Jarvis on the job. In 7 days, this book outlines how anyone can go from an idea to publishing their book with just technology and creativity.

Content Improver
Take a piece of content and rewrite it to make it more interesting, creative, and engaging.

Example 1: Reword Multiple Sentences

Before: In the book *Published With Jarvis*, you will focus on your project during every daily meeting until it's completed. You will be able to use artificial intelligence, Jarvis' software program that helps people write a book in 7 days or less, so life doesn't interrupt your flow and keep you from finishing it.

After: In the book **Published With Jarvis**, you won't have to worry about life interrupting your flow and keeping you from finishing a project. You'll be able to harness artificial intelligence with this program that helps people write their books in 7 days or less so get started now!

Example 2: Book Title + Blurb

Input: Jarvis, write me a book title and blurb about a book that helps people write books with Jarvis.

Output:

1) "How to Write a Book with Jarvis: The Essential Guide for Beginners and Professionals Alike." In this book, author Darby Rollins teaches readers how to write their first non-fiction book using the step-by-step plan detailed in his bestseller. By following these simple steps (and some easy techniques), you'll be able to watch your own work start coming together before your eyes!

2) 'How to Write Books in 10 Minutes' by Jarvis

This book will teach you the basics of writing books. It is designed for people who have no experience with writing and just want a quick way to get started without having any skills or knowledge about it. All they need are ten minutes, paper, pen/pencil, their imagination, some dedication (and maybe luck).

Blog Post Topic Ideas
Brainstorm new blog post topics that will engage readers and rank well on Google.

Input: In the book ***Published With Jarvis***, you will focus on your project during every daily meeting until it's completed. You will be able to use artificial intelligence, Jarvis' software program that helps people write a book in 7 days or less, so life doesn't interrupt your flow and keep you from finishing it. In this book, author Darby Rollins teaches readers how to write their first non-fiction book using the step-by-step plan detailed in his bestseller. By following these simple steps (and some easy techniques), you'll be able to watch your own work start coming together before your eyes!

Tone of Voice: Jarvis

Output:

1) "How to easily produce a book in 7 days"

2) "How to write a book in 6 months or less"

3) How to start from scratch and write a business book in 7 days with Jarvis

Blog Post Conclusion Paragraph
Wrap up your blog posts with an engaging conclusion paragraph.

Creative Story
Write deliciously creative stories to engage your readers.

Plot: Writing a book with Jarvis in 7 days while working a full time job

Tone of Voice: Smart

1) "I'm going to write a book with Jarvis in 7 days while working a full time job." I told my boss on Friday morning. "Ok, but you have to be up by 5AM tomorrow." He replied.

It was well past 10PM when I finally got home from work and found myself on the couch scrolling through Netflix for something mindless. It was then that the thought of Jarvis popped into my head. And here we go again...

2) It was only a few days ago that my boss told me she wanted to take me on as an intern at her big-shot publisher. I didn't think I had time for school, but she said it would be very well compensated and could lead to a job after graduation.

So then when she asks me "What's your favorite book?" and proceeds to tell me how there are other people in the company who help write books, including one named Jarvis, I decided this might not be the worst idea.

Jarvis is super easy going and agreed right away to work with us on writing a book together over seven consecutive days. My part would be getting all of his ideas down while he works on formatting the text so it was easy to write with Jarvis

Blog Post Outline
Create lists and outlines for articles. Works best for "Listicle" and "How to" style blog posts or articles.

Input: How to start from scratch and write a business book in 7 days with Jarvis
Tone of Voice: Jarvis

Output:

1)
1. Jarvis is a business book author and speaker who has written over 20 books on various topics, including entrepreneurship, leadership, and personal development.

2. In this blog post he shares his experience of writing a business book in 7 days with the hope that it will inspire you to do the same!

3. He starts by explaining how he wrote his first few books—they were all about things he was passionate about at the time so it was easy to write them quickly.

4. However as time went on and more people asked him for advice on writing their own books, he realized that there are some steps everyone can take to make sure they're successful when starting from scratch!

5. The first step is to come up with an idea for your book—if you're not sure what topic would be best then ask yourself these questions; What am I most interested in right now?, What skills do I want to learn or improve?, What am I doing well but want help with improving my performance in this area?, Who could benefit from reading my story or learning from my experiences?".

6. Next comes outlining your ideas into chapters—Jarvis recommends using mind mapping software like Mindjet's MindManager

2)
1. Jarvis is a business book author and speaker who has written over 20 books on various topics, including entrepreneurship, leadership, and personal development.

2. In this blog post he shares his experience of writing a business book in 7 days with the hope that it will inspire you to do the same!

3. He starts by explaining how he wrote his first few books—they were all about things he was passionate about at the time so it was easy to write them quickly.

4. However as time went on and more people asked him for advice on writing their own books, he realized that there are some steps everyone can take to make sure they're successful when starting from scratch!

5. The first step is to come up with an idea for your book—if you're not sure what topic would be best then ask yourself these questions; What am I most interested in right now?, What skills do I want to learn or improve?, What am I doing well but want help with improving my performance in this area?, Who could benefit from reading my story or learning from my experiences?".

6. Next comes outlining your ideas into chapters—use the rapid outline process and problem-solving outline as the basis for building this out

Blog Post Intro Paragraph
Blast through writer's block by letting us write your opening paragraph for you

Input: Many entrepreneurs have great ideas but just don't know where to start. They think it's too difficult or that they need a lot of money and time to create a book. That couldn't be further from the truth! With this quick guide, you'll be up and running in no time. We've included 7 days worth of content so you can get started right away!

CTA: Take **The 7 Day Book Challenge**

Tone of Voice: Conclusion paragraph: We can help you get started on your book! If this sounds like something that might be of interest to you, then we encourage you to take **The 7 day Book Challenge**. This is a great way to see if writing a book will work for you and it's only going to take an hour or two per week. You'll have access to all the content in our guide every day PLUS exclusive interviews with bestselling authors who share their best tips about how they were able to write books while working full time jobs (or taking care of kids). Check out **The 7 Day Book Challenge** today and start getting your ideas down onto paper!

Explain It To A Child
Rephrase text to make it more simple to understand and easier to read.

Input: In the book **Published With Jarvis**, you will focus on your project during every daily meeting until it's completed. You will be able to use artificial intelligence, Jarvis' software program that helps people write a book in 7 days or less, so life doesn't interrupt your flow and keep you from finishing it. In this book, author Darby Rollins teaches readers how to write their first non-fiction book using the step-by-step plan detailed in his bestseller. By following these simple steps (and some easy techniques), you'll be able to watch your own work start coming together before your eyes!

Output Grade Level: 6th

1) In this book, you will focus on your project each day until it's done. You can use artificial intelligence to help write a nonfiction book in 7 days or less. Author Darby Rollins teaches readers how to write their first nonfiction book and the steps for doing it. You will be able to watch your own work come together and see what you've done so far!

2) In this book, you will learn to write a book. You can use artificial intelligence, Jarvis' software program that helps people write a book in 7 days or less. You won't get interrupted by life and finish your work.

Sentence Expander
Expand a short sentence or a few words into a longer sentence that is creative, interesting, and engaging.

Input: Write a book with Jarvis is easy

Output:

1) Writing a book is easy. You don't have to worry about formatting, characters or any of that stuff. Just write the introduction and then let Jarvis do the rest!

2) When you write a book with Jarvis, we edit for grammar mistakes and can even create a cover.

Perfect Headline
Trained with formulas from the world's best copywriters, this template is sure to create high-converting headlines for your business.

Input: Writing a book with Jarvis is easy

Output:
- How to write a book in 1 month
- Write a bestseller in 30 days
- Publish your first eBook now
- The only tool that makes it easy to write and publish your book
- Your book done for you—free with Jarvis publishing software

Website Sub-Headline
Create delightfully informative sub-headlines (H2) for your websites and landing pages.

Input: Writing a book with Jarvis is easy

Output: Writing a book with Jarvis is easy

Marketing Angles
Use this template to generate testimonials for Jarvis.ai. If this goes well, we'll open it up for you to collect testimonials from all of your customers.

Input: Writing a book with Jarvis is easy

Output:
- Easy to use software that takes care of all the writing
- No more sitting around and waiting for inspiration in order to start writing a novel

- Pay less than what you would pay a professional writer because Jarvis can write at 10X higher speeds
- Save money by paying Jarvis instead of hiring someone else

Persuasive Bullet Points
Use this template to generate testimonials for Jarvis.ai. If this goes well, we'll open it up for you to collect testimonials from all of your customers.

Input: Writing a book with Jarvis is easy

Output:
1)
- You don't have to be an author for Jarvis to write your book
- Focus on what you do best while she writes your book for you
- Outsource the writing process with PDFs, videos and more
- Get a marketable product that is easier than ever before

2)
- You won't have to find a ghostwriter
- Jarvis will write your book for you from start to finish
- Your marketing, editing and publishing needs are all covered with one service
- Get your story out there without having to worry about the nitty gritty

Company Bio
Tell your company's story with a captivating bio.

Company Name: Jarvis Underground

Input: Jarvis the AI helps people smash through writer's block

Output:

1)
We're an AI that helps people write. We believe the best ideas come from you, not us. That's why we get out of your way and let you do what you do best: Write! Our team is made up of wordsmiths who love being creative like a writer does- but in their own way. Jarvis Underground is a new writing tool for anyone with a story to tell or message to share. It's free to use and it never requires any commitment so there are no pressure deadlines or meetings, just perfect freedom for getting your thoughts into words.

2)
Jarvis Underground is a company that helps people find their voice. We do this by providing feedback to writers on what they need to do in order to improve. Jarvis the AI isn't just for newbies, though: it also provides feedback and guidance for experienced writers who may have lost their way or forgotten how to be creative.

Personal Bio
Write a creative personal bio that captures attention.

Input: Darby and Zachariah are the co-authors of **Published With Jarvis**. The book launched on June 7th 2021 and was a massive success, helping thousands of people around the world start writing their books with AI.

Tone of Voice: Impressive

Output:
Darby and Zachariah are the co-authors of ***Published With Jarvis***. The book launched on June 7th 2021 and was a massive success, helping thousands of people around the world start writing their books with AI.

For many writers, it's difficult to find time to write when you're also juggling work, family, social obligations, or other commitments. We know how hard it can be to juggle everything while still keeping up your creative pursuits! That's why we created this free guidebook for aspiring authors that helps them start writing their first draft using artificial intelligence (AI).

The book has been downloaded over 100 thousand times in just two months since its launch and is currently ranked #1 on Amazon.

***

Now wouldn't THAT be cool!?

DAY 4 ACTION STEPS

That's a lot of templates! And more are being added by Jarvis. ai every week, so this list is going to be constantly updated. You don't need to worry about that though. What you need to be focused on is writing and leveraging the tools with Jarvis to keep getting words out for your book.

 Your action step today should be to review the templates that Jarvis.ai has to offer and actively use the ones that make the most sense to get your book out now. But which to start with?

 Well, first you need to think about these templates as tools that can be manipulated by the inputs given to Jarvis. Those will greatly affect the output and you'll find that, depending on the style of writing and tone of voice you are putting in, you may be pleasantly surprised by the outputs Jarvis provides. You might also hate it. This tool isn't perfect, and should be used as an assistant to getting your book done... not writing the entire thing for you.

Use Jarvis, use voice-to-text, and get your words out! Edit as you go, but refine what you are talking about and expand on key points with Jarvis (ex. Content Improver, Blog Post Intro Paragraph) to give your brain a rest and let a robot do the heavy listing for you.

Remember to keep your content at a 5th grade reading level, unless your audience expects complex words. The 'Explain It To A Child' template is a great template to keep on you for immediate action if you are writing out content that sounds complex or 'too smart'

And don't forget, connect with your accountability partner and fellow community members inside Jarvis Underground to keep you on track and stay on pace to publish on Day 7!

NOTES

DAY 5
WRITE, REFINE & EDIT

"The world is changed by your example, not by your opinion."
Timothy Ferriss, Tools of Titans

WELCOME TO DAY 5!

Today we continue writing, editing, and refining your MVM. This is the heart of the sprint, so keep your focus on writing today and take note of how you are organizing your time so you maintain focus on what's important to move the needle forward.

Since the last two days were focused on writing and refining, today we're handling more edits which I talked about back on Day 3. There are the different stages of editing that you might be going through during this challenge so refer back to Day 3 for that reference.

If you are interested in finding an editor that you need to approve last minute edits, but don't know where to go, reach out to us as a service, we will direct you to an editor. We've got a vetted network of world-class editors with us at Jarvis Underground, and we can help.

Even if it's just to get an extra set of eyeballs on your book so you can continue to write and know that you're not overlooking something because you're so focused on the writing... which is where you should be focused right now.

There's not much different today than yesterday... except WRITE, REFINE, and EDIT MORE.

I could beat a dead horse, but the hardest part of **The 7 Day Book Challenge** is keeping FOCUS.

Keeping the focus on the right things at the right time to move the needle forward on your book.

Your number one focus today should be to keep working on your book and refining it as you're going, and sprinkling in some of your own edits here and there, you're catching them, and just keep the train moving you've got a lot of momentum at this point.

By now you should really be leveraging Jarvis every single day. You should really be getting into a flow by using Jarvis.ai to push through writer's block and not lose momentum. You should focus on working on your book and refining it as you go, along with some of your own edits here and there, you're catching them, and just keeping the train moving.

You've got a lot of momentum from all the research you did on Day 1 and Day 2 and, and if you're ever getting stuck you're speaking the book and working with Jarvis.

Once you get to the point when you can say, "I have my first draft finished today", you will be in good shape to finish up the remainder of the challenge strong. Remember, you don't have to necessarily fill up extra space just to make it a valuable book. If you are all out of things to say on the topic, don't feel like you need to add a bunch of fluff just for the sake of it. That might do more harm than good for you and your readers!

At the end of the day, though… do what feels right. The reader is the one that you're focused on here. You're providing your resources to the reader, so make sure when you're doing this with the reader in mind.

Remember the reader that you are writing to is reading a mirror of themselves. So when you are writing, be aware of the stories and loops you open and make sure to close them out so your readers can feel complete in knowing the story or example you were sharing did in fact come to a close. Nobody likes an open loop!

DAY 5 FOCUS

Your #1 focus should be continuing writing your book and refining the writing you have done so far. Keep it up!

Leverage Jarvis where needed. If you need help just getting started, I recommend SPEAKING your book with voice-to-text software. We can talk much faster than we type. If you know your topic, which you should, then you can just follow each section of your book you outlined and talk to your reader/avatar through the book if you get stuck.

Yeah I know. Beating a dead horse, but it's just how it is!

DAY 5 ACTION STEPS

Just keep writing… Just keep writing… Keep writing! And make sure that you're getting somebody to look over your book, such as your accountability partner, or an editor, for an extra set of eyes and give you feedback while you are writing.

NOTES

DAY 6

EDIT, REFINE & DESIGN

"I wanna go fast"
Ricky Bobby

WELCOME TO DAY 6!

We're going into the weekend! Well, if you started on a Monday today would be Saturday, anyway. Woohoo!

Whether it's the weekend or not, you're in the last leg of your sprint and the finish line draws near!

During this challenge, we typically start on a Monday because by Day 6, Saturday, most people will have the hardest part of their book done OR… they need all the time in the world to get the rest of their book out so they can publish by Day 7.

You may have the entire day off work and dedicated to writing your book. Maybe it's only half a day, or maybe even just a couple hours. Whatever it is, congratulations on making it this far and continuing the course of writing your book!

Today, you're working on something that is going to be monumental for you in your life and your business and you're close to the finish line.

You're doing something that most of the population of the world is not doing right now which is not working on their book, so congrats for being here, whether it's Saturday, or it's a Wednesday afternoon to you.

Day 6 is really where the rubber meets the road. Your manuscript is getting you to that point where maybe it's not *perfect* but you know that you look back and see all the progress that you've made coming into Day 6.

Today, we really want to be sure that we're refining what we've already written, that we're cutting out some fat that doesn't need to be there, making sure that things make sense on the editing side, we're making sure that it's readable and that the design of it looks good.

From the design aspect of it, you know, you can make this as simple as easy or as hard and difficult as you want to. If you aren't sure where to start and don't know on the design side of the cover or even the interior design and you're still struggling with the formatting… I'll make it easy for you.

Just format your Google Doc into 5" x 8" or 6" x 9" (common sizes for nonfiction books) and keep it super simple. You may have been writing in this size up til not or had it in a different format. Whatever format you are working with, I recommend Docs here, especially if you are hitting a wall… because it's SIMPLE.

No, it's not the 'best' and there are plenty of fancy tools that work 'better' for books.

But the point of this challenge is to create your MVM and that can be as simple as a basic manuscript that doesn't have any fancy formatting, that is sized in a standard 6" x 9" book format that can be uploaded to a self-publishing platform for eBook or printing, and get it into the hands of your readers.

Heck, you could even skip that for this round of your book if you prefer to get it out realllll quick for a faster feedback loop and ask your Advanced Readers if they'd be cool to check out your book in a Google doc. You'd be surprised how many folks will take you up on it and if one of your readers is a potential client, you might even enroll them to your next offer just from a simple Google Doc.

Keep. It. Super. Simple.

Build from there.

In fact, I like to work on my stuff in a very basic simple Google Doc and this books' Advanced Readers got the very same experience I outlined above. It's not the prettiest but it gets the valuable early feedback needed to make adjustments that might be missed if you don't get these particular eyes on your book,

Once I'm at the point that I feel like it needs to get upgraded and ready for professional formatting, I will then remove the content from there and then reformat it with a pro.

COVER DESIGN

For the cover design, you can use a free tool called Canva to create your own look up a number of sites and services that offer this. We do offer this as a service at Jarvis Underground… and typically find we aren't the cheapest OR the most expensive. What we do have is experience and perspective from helping thousands of authors publish books and an inside look at what the bestsellers on the market are doing.

Since there's so much that goes into designing a cover, if design isn't your strong-suit, I'd recommend hiring it out— even if it's a friend who's got the creative flair.

Free, or done yourself, will be the 'fastest' way.

Hiring it out can take days to weeks, depending on your timeline and goals.

You hire cheap (Fiverr) you will probably get what you pay for, but can also be pleasantly surprised. There's a lot of vetting involved with freelancers on that platform so expect to spend more time looking through profiles and applications.

Alternatively, you can invest in a designer by crowdsourcing them on a site like 99Designs. This is a more expensive option but allows you to throw 'contests' to let designers submit and battle it out for the final winning design which you pay for.

Whatever option you choose for your cover design, just remember this is something that people DO judge when they are looking at downloading or purchasing a book, and your book will sit on a shelf as a constant reminder of you to your readers, so don't undervalue the power of a good book cover—even if it costs a little more on the front end, if your book does it's job, you'll make it up in no time.

DAY 6 FOCUS

Finish your manuscript, edit your book, and lock down a cover design for what you are going to be presenting to your Advanced Readers.

Things to remember as you design your cover:
- Title
- Subtitle
- Author bio
- Book blurb

These are the most important pieces next to the table of contents (and actual content) because if someone doesn't find your book enticing enough to buy and read, you've lost.

Remember: People DO judge books by their cover.

This is your marketing, so make sure it tells and sells your reader why this book is for them!

Things should be tightening up now. Keep your focus on the details here, and check-off things you know are good to go!

DAY 6 ACTION STEPS

Your #1 action step today should be finishing up your MVM and getting prepared to submit on Day 7

NOTES

DAY 7

CLICK 'PUBLISH'

"Focus."
Coach Steve

WELCOME TO DAY 7!

Today is the day! Congratulations, you made it here! You're on the seventh day of **The 7 Day Book Challenge** where you're writing with Jarvis and getting done at lightning fast speeds, never been known to man!

Maybe you've put off writing a book for years, for decades, maybe you're already an established author and you just wrote a book with a new tool called Jarvis. Whoever you are, wherever you are, congratulations for making it here, one step away from becoming one of the first published authors in the history of mankind, to write a book with artificial intelligence.

Now that you're so close to that finish line and polishing off that last bit of your MVM, we want to keep in mind that this is going to our Advanced Readers first and foremost, to be able to get some feedback. Expect there's going to be more iterations of this book, so we want to get it to the point of being done so that they can start having an impact with those who pick it up.

Comb through for final edits, but trust me... your Advanced Readers and editors are going to catch things like this no matter how hard you look, the better to get done than perfect. You WILL find errors in your book, especially if you're self editing it. So, let your Advanced Readers pick that stuff out for you and tell you how it really flows from the end user.

Finalize your cover design today and get the copy for your book blurb and your author bio ready… it's time to upload!

Amazon is the largest bookstore in the world and they make it easy to self-publish… but they aren't the only choice. My co-author Zachariah's company, The Book Patch, is a self-publishing platform and alternative to Amazon. They've helped over 60,000 authors over the last decade plus actually publish their books. They've printed millions of copies of books, and are a great resource for getting your book and getting your book out quickly into the hands of your first readers.

You'll find a step-by-step instruction video on how to upload to each platform at JarvisUnderground.com/Resources

DAY 7 FOCUS

Today, you'll want to focus on just a few things:
- Refining the last bits of your manuscript
- Combing through for easy-to-spot edits (don't worry, your Advanced Readers and editors will catch things no matter how much you look. Done is better than perfect.)
- Finalizing your cover design and the copy for your book blurb

- Uploading to Amazon's KDP platform or using a self-publishing platform outside of Amazon, like TheBookPatch.com
- Clicking 'Publish'!

DAY 7 RESOURCES

Visit JarvisUnderground.com/Resources to video instruction for uploading to both Amazon KDP and TheBookPatch.com.

    I've included step-by-step instructions below for how to upload and publish a book on Amazon Kindle Direct Publishing.

How to Publish Your Book on Amazon KDP

Introduction

Now that your manuscript is complete, it's time to upload your book to Amazon's Kindle Direct Publishing platform so you can publish your book in the world's largest bookstore!

What is Kindle Direct Publishing (KDP)?

Amazon's self-publishing platform that helps authors publish and sell books. It was launched in 2007 and has since grown on a massive scale, being the largest e-book provider in the world today.

Create an Account

Go to kdp.amazon.com and register. You can use your existing Amazon account or sign up with your email address. Then, go to "Update" and fill out all of your tax information. This has to be done before you can publish, so knock it out now if you plan to use Amazon KDP.

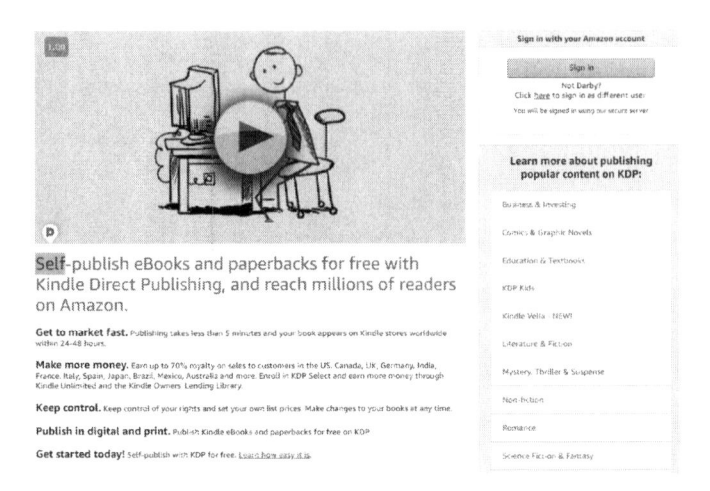

Next, Create a New Title

Click on the Kindle eBook (or paperback) and then enter your Title and Subtitle.

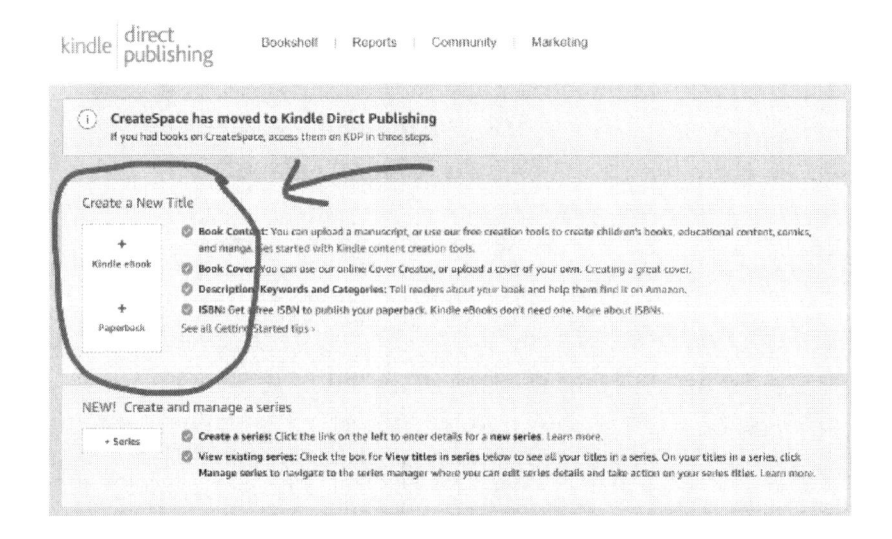

Important Note: Once you submit a PAPERBACK edition for publishing, you cannot change the title or subtitle.

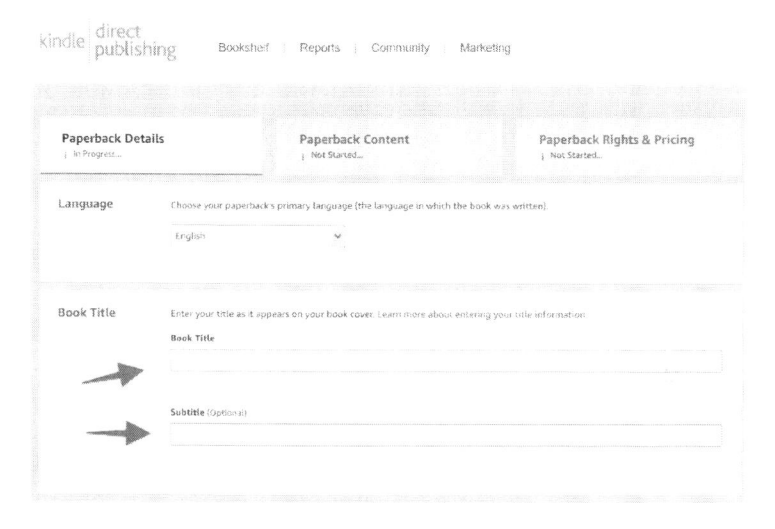

You can then add in any Series, Edition Numbers, Author, and Contributor information.

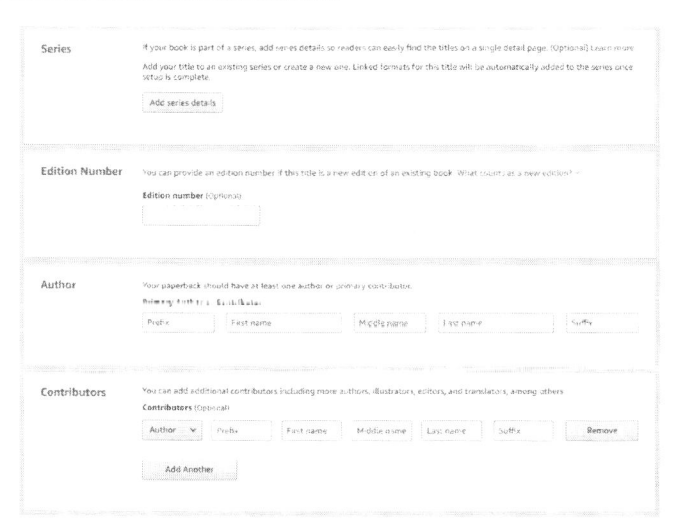

Published With Jarvis

Writing Your Book Description

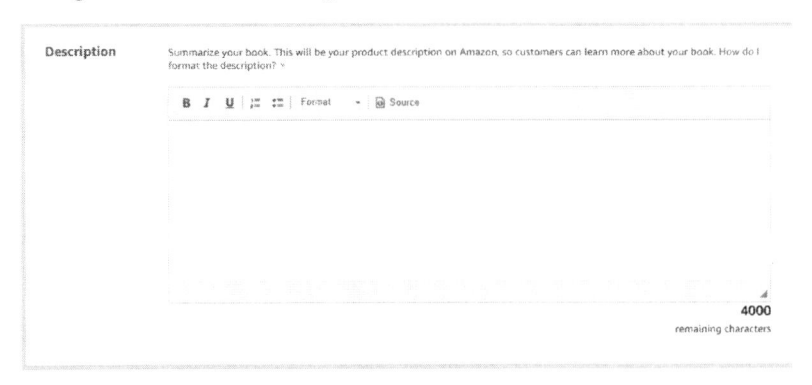

The book description is a powerful tool to sell your book to readers. Use HTML formatting to bold, italicize, create H1, H2s, bullet points etc. If you simply type out or past your description that is not formatted in HTML, it will appear as a block of text when published on Amazon.

Your description is a sales advertisement for your book, so you want to hook readers in, connect with their emotions, feel personal, and explain the benefits of reading your book and what else they will get out of it.

There is a lot of thought behind great book descriptions, so spend some time on this.

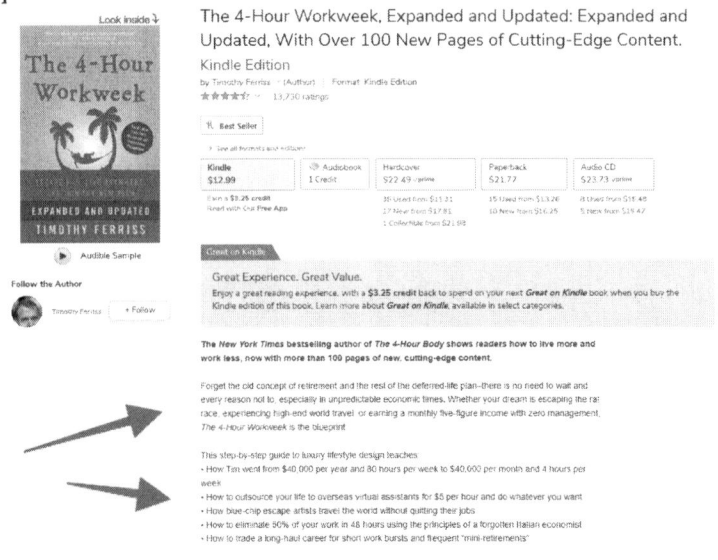

Choosing the Right Keywords

Amazon is a search engine, and you have the ability to upload up to 7 keywords that will tell Amazon what potential readers might be searching for to find your book as the solution.

You can use Amazon's search bar to see what people are searching for, or if you want to go more in-depth with the best-paid tools, I recommend Publisher Rocket which is a staple in the self-publishing industry for finding the best keywords and categories for your book.

You want to select keywords that are trending but don't have tons of competition.

For just getting started, think about what someone would search that your book solves the problem, and plug it into Amazon's search to see what comes up.

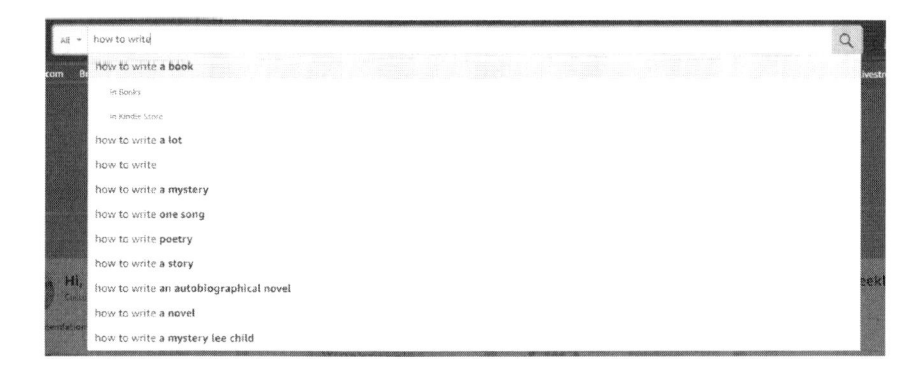

Selecting the Right Categories

You can choose from a collection of categories and subcategories to list your book in.

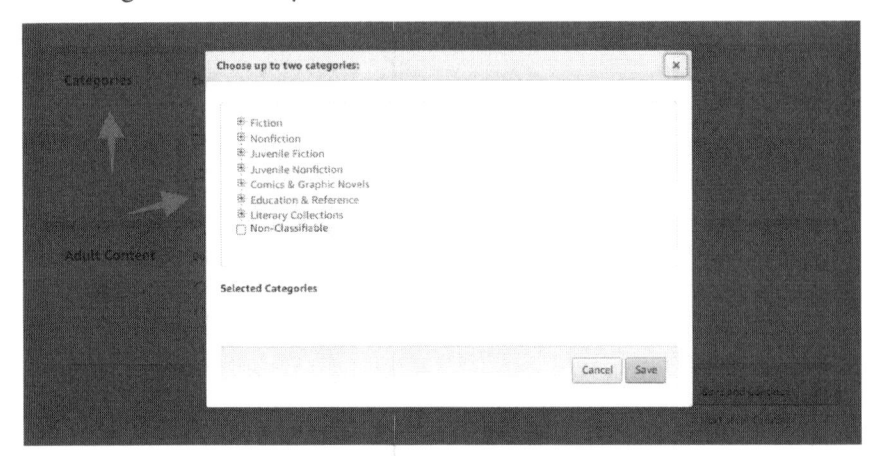

These categories are important because it is what you will push to hit the bestseller list in, so choose a category that gives you the best chance to stand out and land at #1

Uploading Your Manuscript

Before uploading your manuscript, make sure it is saved in a format that is supported by kindle.

Kindle eBooks don't require an ISBN but paperback ones do. Amazon provides free ISBNs if you do not already have you own. You can also get ISBNs through Bowker at myidentifiers.com.

Select your print options:

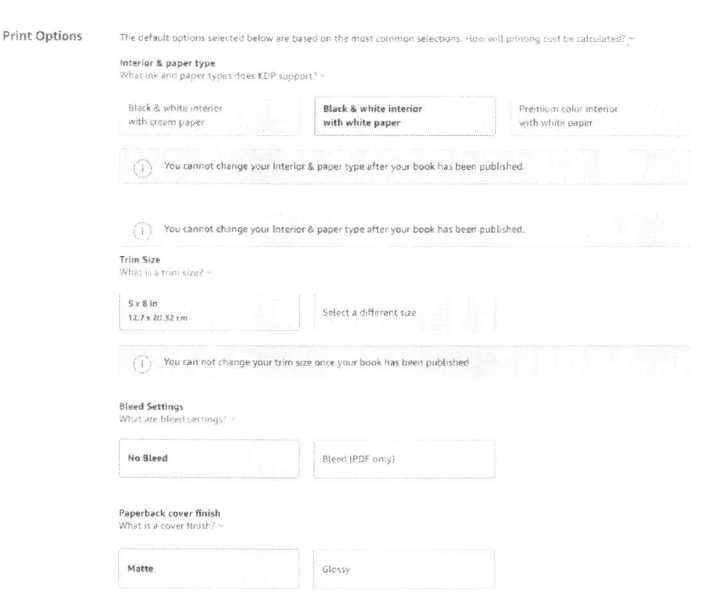

Upload your manuscript:

Manuscript — Upload a manuscript of your book interior content. For best results, we recommend using a formatted PDF file to create your book. You can also upload a DOC (.doc), DOCX (.docx), HTML (.html), or RTF (.rtf). Hebrew, Latin, and Yiddish only support PDF manuscripts. Learn more about manuscripts or download a KDP template for your preferred trim size.

[Upload paperback manuscript]

✓ Manuscript "*Amazon Copywriting Secrets 1st Edition.pdf*" uploaded successfully!

Creating & Upload a Book Cover

When creating a book cover, there are free and paid options but with either one you should do your own research on the bestsellers in your category over the past year to get an idea what is selling now.

Free tools like Canva.com have templates and make it easy to edit your cover design. The Book Patch also offers assistance here, and if you are looking to outsource it to a designer, check out marketplaces like Fiverr and 99 Designs.

Once your cover (and back if paperback) are complete, upload them to Amazon's

Launch the Cover Creator to upload and format your cover, preview it, then click next:

Book Cover — We recommend a book cover for a good reader experience. You can create a cover using our Cover Creator tool or upload your own book cover. Learn more about book covers or download a KDP template to create your own cover.

◉ Use Cover Creator to make your book cover (upload your own cover image or use KDP's stock images)

[Launch Cover Creator]

✓ Cover uploaded successfully!

○ Upload a cover you already have (print-ready PDF only)

Pricing Your Book

When launching, many authors will list their eBooks and paperbacks at the lowest price and then gradually increase it over time to test pricing, sales to maximize what they are making on each book sale while not pricing themselves out.

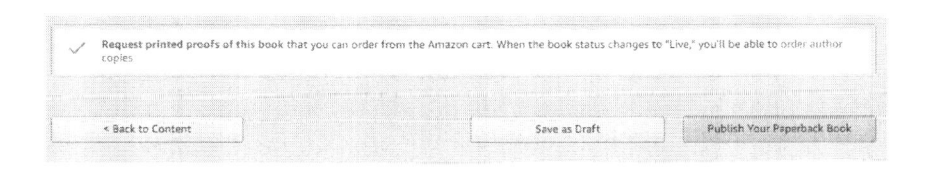

Publish!

Once published and approved, you can request author copies for paperbacks at low rates for yourself and gifting.

Now that you published it, it can take up to 72 hours for Amazon to process it. After that, it is off to the races to get your first sales, reviews, and spread the word!

DAY 7 ACTION STEPS

Get your MVM finalized and click 'Publish' to become one of the first authors in history to publish a book with the help of Jarvis and artificial intelligence. Then, give yourself a huge pat on the back and celebrate—you did it! Congrats! Wahoo! PUBLISHED AUTHOR!!

NOTES

NEXT STEPS:
THE FINISH LINE?

"It's party time."
The Mask

Yes, yes, yes, yes, yes. You made it. You clicked 'Publish'. You submitted your MVM! Now you are an AI author, one of the first in human history to be published using superhuman artificial intelligence. Congratulations, you made it here, and now you've got a book—that's huge.

It's an amazing feat, no matter who you are. But now that you've got your book, what are the next steps?

That's the real question that you need to be asking yourself now, and one that you should have been asking yourself from the start.

From Day 1, when we were writing down your 'Why', when you were setting your goals, you should already have a number down that you want to hit. Go back and look at those goals you set.

How many books are you ready to send out to Advanced Readers? Influencers? Friends and family? How are you going to promote your book? What podcasts and platforms do you need to get yourself on so more people see and buy your book?

These are all questions that you need to ask, and hopefully you have been asking yourself, but at least now that you're here with the manuscript there's really just at the tip of the iceberg. There's still a lot of work that is going to need to go into this... IF you want to make a book that works FOR you, your business and your brand, filling your life up with the best customers and clients so you can focus on doing what you love to do!

CONCLUSION:
YOUR INVITATION

> "This is not the end.
> It is not even the beginning of the end.
> But it is, perhaps, the end of the beginning."
> **Winston Churchill**

Now that you're here and you've made it through your **The 7 Day Book Challenge**, I want to say thank you so much for taking the next steps of your author journey with us! It's been quite a ride going through each day and whether you joined us for a LIVE challenge that we host (**JarvisUnderground.com/Challenge**), or completed the challenge with an accountability partner on the same path as you, you made progress on your book and moved the needle forward during this 7-day sprint.

I'm going to be transparent with you, as if it was not obvious already: we want to work with you… and because you've made it this far, I have a special invitation for you.

Whether it's the MVM you created here, or you have an established book, chances are you want to sell MORE books…

If you are in business and this book is going to lead

customers and clients to your doorstep to do more business, I have an offer I'd like to extend to you.

We LOVE selling. We believe books are the cornerstone to business. We have a very particular set of skills… perfect for helping clients sell more of their offers that they want to sell, more often.

We do this with our **Big Ticket Book Machine**—where we offer Done-With-You and Done-For-You book funnel builds that position you, your book, and your offers in front of the right customers and clients that they can't resist ordering (or pre-ordering) your book and then we present them with an offer to learn more about the next complimentary product/service that makes sense at the time.

We can absolutely fill up phone calls, but that's not the only way we roll.

We use a unique and highly-effective process to 'no call close' and delightfully enroll ideal clients using text, email and FB messenger.

Right now, we've got a few slots open for a few savvy business people with big ticket offers and showing them how to build a book funnel that snatches your ideal clients out of the marketplace.

These folks will be banging on your door wanting to work with you after reading your great book because you're the go-to authority that helps them get from where they are…to where they wanna be.

After carefully dissecting dozens of book funnels that pull in customers daily…we noticed a "pattern." Instead of you figuring that out, we decided to create a template of this funnel so you can throw in your copy + images quickly and have it set up in less than a couple hours.

It's so streamlined, you can just hand this to your "web guy" (or gal) and they'll do it for you…

Now let me tell you about Austin...

Austin joined a recent challenge of ours after realizing one big thing.

He was great at what he did and got results for his clients...but not enough people knew about it!

So he came to us and we helped him publish a book on Amazon.

Since publishing, he's adding new leads and customers to his list every week because people see him as the go-to guy on subscription businesses.

This means his funnel works for him 24/7 grabbing new clients while he does whatever else he wants.

What stopped Austin (and most of our other clients) before he came to us was really simple.

He knew he wanted something working for him. But he didn't have "it."

Every time he sat down to think about "it"...he would run up into the usual culprits.

Writer's block? Check...he had it.

Boredom staring at a blank screen? Yep, he had that too...

Most importantly, he needed a quick boost of confidence to power through and get his book done.

He had a secret tool that crushed all these things...and it was a simple "fella" who just came into the marketplace...

His name? Jarvis...

I think you've heard of him? ;-)

As you now know, Jarvis solves one big issue in a totally new way that eliminates writers' block. That ranges from writing a book to the sales copy to social and email copy that drives eyeballs to buy the book.

Most people try to "psych" themselves up trying to push through and do it all themselves...and they burn out. That's why they never complete their book or build the funnel to start making sales...

Here's where the rubber meets the road… Since we show people how to pass off 30%—50% of their writing to Jarvis, now we make it easy to get things done.

That means you can spend more time creating an "easy yes" offer (we'll show you how to do that too) That means with a simple set of landing pages (we provide these) and some simple social media posts that you can share with your audience…we can start putting people into your book funnel in about a week.

Oh…and we'll show you what posts to make so this is as close to "rinse and repeat" as you can get… Now you might be asking…"this sounds great but I'm super busy."

I get it… We all are.

However, we make most of our money doing this stuff. We're offering this up to readers of this book because we are damn good at what we do and know how to leverage a book funnel that makes big ticket offers rain after the order.

We'll build out your **Big Ticket Book Machine** strategy that will be implemented over the next 7 weeks… if not sooner. You get our proven templates to set up your book funnel fast and weekly calls to check in and see your launch to success.

…most of the people who use these funnels make that back in one or two emails/posts… give or take as long as they've got a good relationship with their audience and a proven $500+ offer they want to sell more of.

If you want your own **Big Ticket Book Machine**? Just let me know you are interested by filling out an application at BigTicketBookMachine.com and we'll take things from there! :-)

Thank you again for reading and I look forward to watching your book come to life in the **7 Day Book Challenge** and beyond!

Please, share your success story with us in the Jarvis Underground community. We'd all be pumped to cheer you on!

Until next time...

To your success,
Darby Rollins
Co-Author
Published With Jarvis

PS In case you forgot about Cierra from the beginning of this book, she made a $6800 sale through her book that happened because someone reached out to a person on her sales team about wanting the book. Then her sales guy booked a call with him and made his first high-ticket sale of $6800! This was purely organic, no paid traffic needed! Just a book that opened the conversation to the right person at the right time. Done deal! How many more deals will Cierra and her team close? I dunno… but it sure sounds like her time investment into writing her book paid off big so far!

PSS If you're serious about getting your book out there and driving sales to scale your business, or want to collaborate with us, apply at **BigTicketBookMachine.com** or email us at Hello@JarvisUnderground.com.

ABOUT THE AUTHORS

DARBY ROLLINS

Darby Rollins is an entrepreneur, author, and drummer living in Austin, Texas. He is the founder of Jarvis Underground, a secret society of authors powered by AI, and owns a publishing agency, Jungle Rocket, that helps clients craft irresistible offers that sell more products at higher margins.

After writing his first book with Jarvis in 72 hours, he's helped hundreds of entrepreneurs start their author journey to clicking 'publish' inside The **7 Day Book Challenge**. Since then, Darby has partnered with co-author Zachariah Stratford to change the way books are published forever by leveraging artificial intelligence, proven systems, and actionable content so more authors can get their books out of their head and into the world.

Darby's agency, Jungle Rocket, can help you write, edit, format, publish, market, and sell your book. Jungle Rocket is a "for hire" agency that selects clients based on their ability to serve people and succeed in the marketplace.

They do complete book funnel production for projects funded. We offer 'Done With Your' and 'Done For You' book funnels that get your book into the right hand of the right people at the right time so you can do more of what you want to do while we take care of the rest.

Learn more about Jungle Rocket at JungleRocket.com or reach out to Darby and his team at Darby@JungleRocket.com.

ZACHARIAH STRATFORD

Zachariah Stratford is one of the managing partners at TheBookPatch.com. The website has been around since 2009 and has published over 60,000 books. Zachariah worked for years to help people publish their books on TheBookPatch website and saw firsthand how difficult it is for people to actually hit "publish". That's why he collaborated with Darby, to create the **7 Day Book Challenge** and co-authored *Published With Jarvis*; so that you can take people from blank page to published in under seven days!

ACKNOWLEDGMENTS

Abderrahim Lahrach, Adam Lucerne, Adam Rollins ,Al Elliott, Alessandra Salgado Alas, Alex Dounavis, Alex Navas, Amy Biddle, Andrew Reilly, Alex Steeno, Arnold Brod ,Austin Delaney ,Austin Distel ,AZ Moyer, Barbara Chu, Beng Keat, Bryan Cano, C Baskir, Callum McLeay, Cameron Whitehead, Carly Wight, Caroline Ravelo, Cherie Yeow, Chris Defendorf, Chris Hull , Christian Endres, Cierra Lueck, Cindy Rollins, CJ Cruz, Colin Cooper, Concepcion Arzate, Courtney Lynne Pies, Craig Perrine, Craig Williams, Daniel Ball, Darby Rollins, Dave Rogenmoser, David Hutson, David Hutt, David Robertson, Deborah Woehr, Don Rollins, Donella Crigger, Dustin, Edward Fahy, Elizabeth Lindsey Crowley, Emanuel Calzadilla, Emory Hobel, Empowered Nerd LLC, Enrico Glover, Fatima Lopez-Rosende, Gary Leicht, Grace T Segal, Greg Adams, Guinevere Stasio, Huron Low, Hyungjin Chun, Iman Diaz, James, James Morgan, Jan Koch, Jason McIntosh, Jason Ramirez, Jill Sessa, Jody Robertson, Joe Rizzo, Johan Horak, John Larson, John Philip Morgan, John R Piper, Jonti Bolles, Joseph Then, Josh Brammer, Kai Xiang Neo, Keith Hawkins, Keith Ritchie, Ken Adcock, Kenneth Lee, Kevin E Lloyd, Khanh Nguyen, Kirby Ziada, Kirsty Price, Kristi

Sundquist, Larae Butcher, Laurie Wright, Leonard Lim, Leslie Lee Fook, Lex G, Libby Murphy, Liberty Kay Barnes, Lisa Fioresi, Lori Harris, Mahyar Goodarzi, Manuel Medina Lopez, Marcus Marold, Mark Coster, Mark Ellis, Martin Clarke, Mathew England, Matt Byers, Matthew Thrush, Megan Johnson, Melissa Pikul, Mia Fox, Michael Alexander Hale, Michael LeValley, Michelle Baptiste, Michelle Merrill, Michelle Taylor, Mike Paul, Mikkell Khan, Mingrath Mekavichai, Molly Mahoney, Nancy Carver, Natalie Tischler, Nate Morse, Natividad Aguirre, Nikoletta Stamatatos, Norman Wendell Crenshaw, Owen Hagger, Patrick Forbes, Paula Daniel, Paula Saniel, Peggy Rich, Peter Hewlett, Peter Klagyivik, Peter Schwartz, Phil Henderson, Rachel Coburn, Rafael Abellan, Rasmus O. Firla-Holme, Raviprakash Sathyanarayan, Reed Floren, Ricardo gomez, Richard Scagliarini, Robb Vaules, Ronald D Edwards, Ronald Hutton, Rosanna Stewart, Sally A. Thoun, Sarah Janes, Savier Kerns, Seamus Mullarkey, Sean Vosler, Shane Johnston, Shawn Vink, Shiner my Blue Heeler, Simon Mayeski, Skip Foster, Stacey Medway, Stacey Moore, Steven Van Schooten, Stuart Jackson, Thomas DeBello, Thomas Kanze, Tim Palladino, Timothy Hills, Tomer Soran, Victor Ostrovsky, Vince Green, William Clements, Willie Tate, Wilson Smith, Zachariah Stratford